trouvaille

Emily Kennedy

BookLeaf Publishing

India | USA | UK

Presentation by *BookLeaf Publishing*

Web: www.bookleafpub.com

E-mail: info@bookleafpub.com

ISBN: 978-93-5744-980-9

First edition 2022

DEDICATION

For Rory,

Thank you for being my trouvaille.

ACKNOWLEDGEMENT

These poems would not have been possible without the heartfelt support and inspiration I receive from my friends and family. Thank you to Connie, for always encouraging me to write even if I don't feel like it. Thank you to Mona, who floated into my life and inspires me to show up as the best version of myself. And thank you to Rory. For being my kite string, and helping me not fly away completely. Lastly, I thank our Mother Earth, for always providing endless peace and sanctuary in our chaotic society.

PREFACE

Trouvaille is a French word meaning 'a lucky find'.

Rory was my luckiest find in the strangest of times. From him I gained the support and encouragement to continue writing, and through times of pain and sadness came some of my proudest poems. This is my trouvaille.

alchemy

weathered hands and midas touch,
heart of gold and golden hours
try to bring light to the world,
build a home from the ashes
precious skin, handle with care
what i make is divine
alchemy
whatever i touch
turns to gold
whatever i have is bigger
than me.
fire hazard, relentless magnitude
of sparks from within.
don't come too close you'll
burn yourself.
evergreen and flammable
yet soft and tangible.
come see me rebuild myself
from the ground, turning
stone into gold

wish

11:11, make a wish
Shooting stars
A fallen eyelash
And dandelion seeds
Or a lucky penny
Comet tails
Birthday candles
Pulling petals
Love me, love me not
Break the wishbone
See the rainbow
Find a pot of gold
Or a treasure chest
Always wished for
You

23

it took me 23 years
of sorrow, self-loathing and suffering
poetic sibilance, sweet nothings
and hard graft
to realise all along
i'd been searching for a knight
or a princess
but what they didn't teach me
in high school is that
skin is still skin, even if it's thin
my sensitivity is a strength
my dreams are never too big
because after all this time
all i'd ever needed was me
and i am the love
of
    my
        own
           life

roots

the time before you
was restless, ceaseless
writhing and wriggling
chaos and confinement.
a body of anxiety bursting
its banks day after day.
now your presence has
soothed my soul,
quietened even the thoughts
raging with pain.
i breathe comfort and candour
incandescent and aglow.
melting into the earth around us
we are entangling our roots
to make our way back home.
a spectacle to those too scared
of intertwining love and loss,
from roots we make homes
in the earth where we stare
at stars and tether ourselves
to whatever makes us feel
alive.

philosophy

Plato's eight limbs and cartwheels
supernovas and starstuff
an infinite red string, tied to the pinkies
fateful interventions and 'meant to be's
however our souls came to be
if they smashed into one another in the cosmos
or if we've grown old in bodies and died
time and time again to reunite
and feel that homecoming once again
I don't know how it works
how it came to be or where we came from
woken up from a dream
everything is as it should be
can't wrap my head around it
because it is bigger than me and you
it is lightyears wide and brighter than the stars
the feeling that could stop wars
and heal the soul
we might even be changing the world

a soul in water

bring with you respect and courage
when facing her majesty
the sapphire jewel of chaos and calm
eastern light offering sodium sunrises
brings infinite gifts
of coarse geology and a safe home
of sea salt and sea foam
revel in the surf or deep in the depths
enigmatic wonder and glorious breaths
to inhale the power and liquid therapy
to catch the waves and ride the tide
exposed to the elements with
nowhere to hide
let it wash over you
with the energy of the moon
revealed only is truths
as you return to a natural state
of being in a body of water
with crashing waves washing away
the layers of the dull every day
the mundane and ordinary
delight in the world of the momentary
surf, sands and sea glass
feel the fullness in the heart
of the beholder betwixt blue waves

morning dew and evening haze
find a coastline gem to roam
to feel your soul return back home

headspace

pencil to the paper
pedal to the floor
exhale troubles
ignite me to the core.
fuel my need to articulate
my sorrow and my sadness
my happiness and my joy
my delirium and my madness.
be it scrawled in a book
scratched in the sand
or only for my brain to hear
it's a safe space to crash land
my whirring thoughts
and whispers of ideas
those lines on that paper
know all my hopes and fears.
find me under a tree
or hiding under my bed
igniting the paper with
the voices inside my head.
if I don't write it down
they will try and escape
gasping to get out
like a mouth stuck with tape.
ambition and doubt pour out

only at the fingertips
with the awe and wonder
of a solar eclipse.
a parachute of poems
might sometimes land on the page
attempting to mean something
as "all the world's a stage".
a few words in the abyss
without enough time
to note down all the words
but it's my time to shine.

quitter

never could quite commit
to just about anything
cutting a cake and saying
"just a small bit"
because I'm on a diet
at night my stomach riots
fall off the wagon again
try again next monday
only the cycle repeats
the next monday
and the monday after
it's always followed with
shrugging and laughter
because that's the way it is
like it since we were kids
new hobby each week
nothing could pique
my interest longer than 5 seconds
even my mum reckons
I have the attention span of a goldfish
what was I writing about again?
oh right, but even then
nothing seems to stick
tried to learn to knit
even that I quit

with not even a hat to show for it
tried taking up running
that one was funny
thought that one might catch on
time to book a half marathon
broke in my new running shoes
and by then it was old news
bought a pair of rollerskates
and soon my new destiny awaits
and for them I bought new laces
skated round several places
then I started an art business
and for that I ask forgiveness
sold one painting and called it a day
that one wasn't here to stay
then tried my hand at DIY
obviously trying to diversify
sewed a set of curtains
this one I was certain
would stick around for a while
but thinking that was juvenile
swiftly moving on
I headed back to Amazon
to buy sketchpads and oil pastels
and drew sea glass and sea shells
you'd make a Picasso of me yet
though on that I wasn't dead set
either
seems now I understand Plath's fig tree

and in all my beautiful idiosyncrasy
I pick all the figs and make myself sick
and that will always be my party trick

jitters

I have social anxiety
Never have I appropriately
Been able to express my feelings
Without leaving people reeling
Feel my heartbeat in my throat
Wishing I could just float
Away, while people say
Is she okay?
While I remember to breathe
Tugging relentlessly on my sleeve
Exude that false confidence
While quietening my consciousness
Fake it til you make it they say
Brushing all the jitters away
But what if my panic makes me me
And it helps my ability
To sympathise and synthesise
The ever changing world around me
My brain is not broken
It's just timid and quietly spoken
And I'm an anxious kid
Trapped in 24 year old skin
The way it always has been
But I wouldn't change it even if I could
Love myself anyway just the way I should

space suit

under my ribcage
lies a gaping darkness
that swallows everything in its path
all logic and reason
gone
no sign of intelligent life
but a hungry gravity field
gorging itself on doubt and desolation
the void swells and deepens
constricting my bones
choking my airways
poisoned with melancholy
a black hole
with a celestial sadness
and a course set for oblivion
should you look at me
my eyes like telescopes
looking past glassy pupils
at some remnants of life
several lightyears away
a star that once burned
but is many years gone now
just residual light and dust remain
scattered into the ether
an untethered and uncontrollable

trajectory to the abyss
with nothing but a troubled brain
on a flight path to self destruct
skin ready to combust into flames
reducing me to stardust
nothing but atomic matter
perching on a spinning rock
in the infinite universe
just breathe, they say
when it seems impossible
like the air has ceased to exist
and the atmosphere has evaporated
into complete nothingness
that was until
he came along
regulated my breathing
grounded me on solid earth
soothed my burning skin
extinguished the desolate fires
in the deepest caverns of my soul
altered my vision
the perspective no longer askew
saw myself
as the supernova I am
raging with infinite energy
a furnace of intrigue and promise
of greater things to come
marvelled at me
as if any celestial body

was simply a support act
for my mere existence
he was my very own
space suit

shackles

was it part of the master plan
to post your life on Instagram
seeking material validation
for the precise fabrication
of highlight reels
and approval seals
of an online life
that you clutch so close.
keeping up appearances
authentic identity disappearances
one day you'll look back
because you lost track
and started to doubt
that life seldom meant anything
without your follower count.
living each day through a screen
just to feel digitally seen
when the world turns around you
but you're not really living for you,
are you?
you're living for the friends
and acquaintances,
potential love interests
and past bedroom conquests.
living for the hashtag memories

treating moments like accessories
to exaggerate your existence
with admirable persistence.
build up a social media document file
of all the events that make life worthwhile
to demonstrate your success
trying desperately to impress
people you know nothing about
all for social hierarchy clout.
because everybody knows
when it's your time to go
the only way to the afterlife
is followers and Facebook likes
out of all life's feats
most important is retweets
and without them you'd be no one
a social ghost who's been outrun
by someone younger and trendier
equally filled with emptiness.
so take a moment to think
about your life without a link
to a digital universe
where you're not shackled to a device
because it comes at a price
of losing who you are
at an individuality abattoir.

may 7th

glimmering harbour lights
breeze amiss and the sun clinging on
to the friday haze as the night swelled
around what felt like the top of the world
stereo oozes gemini by tash sultana
rain gently masking a teenage heartbeat
time slipping away, eating into early hours
imitating the sun holding onto
the passing of fleeting moments
had I the superpower i'd have stopped time
built a house, grown old
and died in that moment

green thumb

You sowed the seeds of doubt
But I watered them
Saw them bloom
Watched my rebirth from the dirt
Cut a rose bush down to almost nothing
For them to grow back stronger
Guess I had a green thumb after all

endometriosis

Years of anguish, blood, and fear
Please tell me how I'm still stuck here
Waiting rooms and surgical faces
Ruined underwear and dismissed cases
It's all in your head, all for attention
"You realise it's probably just depression?"
Days of blood and torturous demons
Late into the night, relentless screaming
Make it stop, make it all go away
All while, my insides are ablaze
Creatures clawing, gnawing to get out
Barbed wire and stabbing until I blackout
Sleepless nights, awake until dawn
All this extra time for me to dwell-on
The never ending demons who live to torture
I'm disoriented like a lamb for slaughter
Tablets of all different shapes and sizes
In the hopes that one of them quiets
The unrelenting waves of pain and sadness
Which tumble me into a silent madness
Endometriosis is the name of the awful disease
I pray that one day I'll be at ease

freefall

All aboard for the sunset drop
Tangerine skies and sunbeam eyes
Time to face those inner demons
High above the cloud line
10,000 feet and a shaking heart beat
No stranger to fear way up here
Teeter on the edge, holding my breath
And then
Drop
Into freefall
A love affair with gravity
So inexplicably sweet
Revelling in the oxygen saturation
The calm panic and thrilling peace
Doing as the birds do
Spreading my wings
Learning to fly

alone

I don't just burn my bridges,
I demolish them, scorch the moat
And set landmines in the surrounding trenches
I cut strings so irreparably
You won't ever hear from me again
They say that love and loss
Is important to grow
But I'm stronger now and
know how to be alone

poems for the poet

When all words are on the table
Cut open and bleeding inspiration
Until nothing remains
Extracted line by line
From a creative brain
And stuck together like a collage
Of trauma, love and loss
But who then writes
Poems for the poet?
When does she get
A sonnet in return
About golden sunsets
Hazy skies and hazel eyes
Maybe one day the
Others will see the way
She looks at the world
Through those rose-tinted
Glasses
And she'll get one, too.

autumn

stormy nights and broken branches
hot tea and cold hands
steam aswirl and porcelain cups
on chapped lips as a breeze
bitter as it comes
claws at the exposed skin.
full moon and starry nights
fallen leaves like broken dreams
crunch with each step
on hardened earth.
how might one survive
the blackened evenings
and sorrowed sun
lonely and withered flora
to sleep at peace
for just a while
until soon the colours will sprout
the birds will sing again.